In Time — A Ranch

Joel

merry christmas

love Sarah &

03

E.M. Fletcher

Printed in Victoria, Canada

National Library of Canada Cataloguing in Publication

Fletcher, E. M. (Ellen Marie), 1921-
    In time--a ranch / E.M. Fletcher.
ISBN 1-4120-0926-X
    1. Fletcher, E. M. (Ellen Marie), 1921-. 2. Ranch life--British Columbia--Cariboo Region. 3. Cariboo Region (B.C.)--Biography. I. Title.
FC3845.C3Z49 2003   971.1'7503'092   C2003-904844-6

TRAFFORD

This book was published *on-demand* in cooperation with Trafford Publishing.
On-demand publishing is a unique process and service of making a book available for retail sale to the public taking advantage of on-demand manufacturing and Internet marketing. **On-demand publishing** includes promotions, retail sales, manufacturing, order fulfilment, accounting and collecting royalties on behalf of the author.

Suite 6E, 2333 Government St., Victoria, B.C. V8T 4P4, CANADA

Phone	250-383-6864	Toll-free	1-888-232-4444 (Canada & US)
Fax	250-383-6804	E-mail	sales@trafford.com
Web site	www.trafford.com	TRAFFORD PUBLISHING IS A DIVISION OF TRAFFORD HOLDINGS LTD.
Trafford Catalogue #03-1295		www.trafford.com/robots/03-1295.html

10   9   8   7   6   5   4   3   2   1

This book is dedicated to my children, grandchildren and great grandchildren. I thank them all for their encouragement and participation.

With Love, Mom and Grandma Marie

*I would like to acknowledge Fern Hinse,
my editor, without whom this book would
never have been published. Fern has
patiently guided me step by step through the
publishing process. Thank you, Fern, for
your patience, wisdom and friendship.
I appreciate you.*

Marie.

Table of Contents

Chapter I	Conquering the World	1
Chapter II	Those Coarse Blue Overalls	17
Chapter III	Excerpts From Orville's Memoirs	19
Chapter IV	Master's Degree	23
Chapter V	Outgrowing Our First Ranch	35
Chapter VI	144 Mile Ranch	47
Chapter VII	From Roadhouse to Ranch Home	51
Chapter VIII	The Sheep and Why	57
Chapter IX	The Options	69
Chapter X	Irrigation Projects	75
Chapter XI	The Horse That Became Friend and Family	81

FR

CHAPTER 1

Conquering the World

In February of 1931, I observed with some concern my dad taking the 1928 Chevrolet car apart. It seemed to me there were a great number of pieces lying about. I thought, *"How can he ever get all those pieces together again?"*

I liked going places in that car. When we went someplace in the car everyone seemed happier. We talked to one another. We saw interesting places. We went on picnics. Once Dad stole a huge watermelon from a field. I love watermelons. That car was my door to a happier world.

My Dad was a lean, dark-haired, hard working, honest man, despite the watermelon episode. I think I would have liked him if I had ever had a chance to get acquainted. He was working in the Oregon logging woods during my early childhood and seldom came home, and then only briefly.

Dad said he was fixing the car because we were going to Canada.

"We were going to Canada!"

In my not quite ten-year-old eyes Canada was a very foreign northern country many miles away. February seemed a strange time to be going north, but I wasn't worried about that. I was troubled about all those pieces of the car lying around.

The 1928 Chev car that my Dad (in the center) overhauled to make the trip to Canada. *(That is me looking over his shoulder).*

Then came *The Day*. The car had been reassembled; a trailer heavily loaded was hitched to it. The last of the household goods were packed into the car. Thus, bright and early on a February morning, we headed for Canada.

Nettie, my delicate blue-eyed blond sister and I had a good place to ride. We sat in the back seat on top of the bedding where we could watch the scenery go by. My parents hoped a change of climate would help Nettie's health. Me? I was disgustingly healthy. I had big brown eyes and much admired apple red cheeks that I considered an affliction. I wanted to be little and delicate and pale like Nettie but I was sturdy and tanned and mature beyond my years.

A few days later we were battling ice and snow in the Bluit Pass. The road was narrow and winding.

Occasionally the car stalled. With the trailer piled high with household goods it was pulling quite a load. When it stalled it usually slipped back on the ice. Mother had some blocks at her feet. She would jump out and throw one or two behind the wheels. Dad would get out a shovel and find some gravel or dirt and cover the ice. Soon we would be on our way again.

For a frail lady with a weak heart Mother was standing up to a rough trip remarkably well. She was from the largest city in the world—New York. She was the daughter of a well-to-do butcher and had spent the summers of her maiden years on her father's beautiful Virginia farm. From this farm, she eloped with my father, and adventuresome as they were, they travelled by covered wagon to the Oklahoma oil fields.

Later they moved to the Peace River Block in Alberta, then to Montana, then Oregon. After they had moved from Montana to Oregon, Dad came home from the logging camps on the weekends and mother was troubled with an attack almost every time he came home. Now Mother was busy packing. We were moving to the Cariboo District in Central B.C and it had been some time since she had been troubled with a heart attack. That was wonderful!

After conquering the Bluit Pass, road conditions improved.

As we neared the Canadian border, there was very little snow. It had been an unusually cold but dry winter.

"How do we know when we are in Canada?" I asked.

"The Canadians all have red noses," replied Dad.

We entered Canada in the warmer fruit growing area of the Okanagan Valley.

I began looking for red noses. There didn't seem to be any more in Canada than in the U.S.A. I concluded Dad had been fooling me.

The road was gravel and dirt with chuckholes and ruts.

Why didn't they look for their farm in the Okanagan? Perhaps land was cheaper farther north? Perhaps Dad wanted a redder nose?

Anyway, Williams Lake was the chosen land of promise and to Williams Lake we were going.

Eagerly I watched the country slide by. What would be around the next bend or over the next hill? Once out of the Okanagan we were again travelling through snowy country.

I don't recall how long we travelled through B.C.

I do remember—70 Mile House. A cold wind whistled across the barren fields. A thin covering of snow drifted in the wind promising another droughty summer. The country had already suffered a series of dry summers.

We pulled into a weathered little gas station. A lady came to gas up the car. She noted the Oregon license plate.

Upon being told we intended to stay in the country she remonstrated, *"Why in hell would you come to this God-forsaken country? In the winter you will freeze up and bust. In summer you'll dry up and blow away!"*

Well, on we went. We would arrive in Williams Lake that night.

We were travelling along a winding road. Looking out Nettie and I could see either a lake or a deep canyon below us. It was too dark to tell. Then the car sputtered and died.

From Oregon to Williams Lake—*the first night spent here.*

It had done well up to now pulling the heavy trailer and carrying a packed load over all the icy mountains and all the rough pot-holed gravel roads. My dad must have known something about cars.

He jumped out a few tools in hand. A little banging and shaking and back in he hopped, and away we went.

It was Williams Lake that Nettie and I had been looking down on. A few miles farther and there was the town. The population was around 500. There were two hotels. We stayed at the Maple Leaf.

Next morning Mother looked out the hall window. All she could see was a few tarpaper shacks set in the bleakness of a northern February morning. *"I will never like Williams Lake,"* she decided.

By April my folks had bought a small farm ten miles from Williams Lake and a mile out of the little village of 150 Mile House.

There was a little red schoolhouse with 25 pupils from grades one to eight taught by one teacher.

Marie aboard *the wall-eyed pidgeon toed horse* and
Nettie standing beside.

Nettie and I were soon enrolled.

There were also a few dwellings, a store, a post
office, a hotel and the 150 Mile Ranch that ran about 1000
beef cattle.

Soon we had five or six milk cows, chickens, pigs,
and a large vegetable garden.

Mother sold butter, milk, cream, vegetables, eggs,
and fryers. Dad sold firewood and sometimes worked on
ranches in the haying season.

Before school I milked cows and delivered the
milk to people in the 150 Mile House village.

Mother had made a canvas bag that went over my
horse's back. It had pockets in it for the milk bottles, and
I rode on top. I was certain I was a funny looking sight,
with the bottles clanking and my pigeon toed wall-eyed

old horse going as slowly as possible through the village.

I made it more ridiculous by trying to switch him into more action so I could get out of sight quicker.

Nettie couldn't seem to learn to milk a cow or handle a horse or several other chores I had no difficulty with.

I therefore concluded—I was smarter than she.

It took me years to figure out who was smartest.

Sometime during the first year, Mother had borrowed some money from her people in New York to buy a horse-rake and mower. I suspect they had used up all their savings buying the farm and that the income from it was not very much.

Mother began having *heart attacks* again, usually after a discussion regarding taking better care of the machinery her folks had been good enough to lend them money to buy.

No one was talking much anymore. Dad moved into the only other bedroom by himself. Nettie slept with Mother. I slept on a pile of cushions and blankets on the floor of the closet. I liked my seclusion.

Nettie seemed oblivious to the gloom around us.

Orville—a young man who worked for the 150 Mile Ranch became a frequent visitor. With his booming laugh, merry broad lipped smile and twinkling blue eyes, he brightened the atmosphere and tempted me to play tricks on him.

I can see him yet—roaring with laughter when my perfectly executed trick—aimed at him—went astray and landed on my dad instead.

I had hung a pail of water, a good-sized milk pail full, on a nail above the kitchen door—carefully balanced so that the door just caught the bottom of the pail and tipped the water neatly over the unwary person entering.

Only the unwary person who entered *first* was my dad with Orville close behind, but far enough to miss every drop.

My dad gasped! I gasped! Orville leaned against the wall and roared! Orville's laugh was so contageous— even Dad had to laugh.

My parents seemed to enjoy visiting with him. Sometimes he helped my Dad with some farm chore. He often helped me with the milking. Sometimes in the evenings we all played card games. When our eyes met across the table the very air was charged.

How could I resist falling in love? His blue eyes said so plainly; *"I love you."*

But I was only 12—too young to fall in love. He was 23. But fall in love I did.

Mother's health was rapidly deteriorating. The *heart attacks* were more frequent and devastating. Dad's fanning no longer restored her. She was gasping for breath and hyperventilating. Orville arrived one evening and observing her condition called in a Doctor. I wondered why Dad hadn't done that sooner.

Mother was hospitalised.

Orville made arrangements for Nettie and I to stay with neighbours.

I told him about Mother's family in New York and he notified them.

When she was sufficiently recovered, arrangements were made for us to go to her people.

Dad was furious. He said that Orville should mind his own business. The Doctor recommended that she not go back to live with Dad.

My Uncle Joe paid for a first class private compartment

for *our* trip to New York.

I was sad. I didn't want to leave Orville. He held me in his arms and asked me to marry him when I grew up. He said he would come to New York and bring me back.

In June of that year Orville took Nettie, Mother and I, to Ashcroft—the closest railway terminal going east and saw us off for New York City.

The trip through the incomparable Rocky Mountains and across the vast prairies, the one day stop over in Niagara Falls and on to Grand Central Station, New York—should have been an exciting adventure for a 13 year old girl, but my heart and mind were elsewhere.

Orville, the love of my life and the only dependable adult I knew—was gone. At least that's the way I felt about it.

In New York my uncle and aunt were generous in supplying our needs. But I wasn't comfortable being supported by them. I felt I should support myself or my parents should support me.

Nettie seemed happy with the arrangements. She soon became Uncle Joe and Aunt Flora's girl. She lived with them in the fifth floor apartment.

I lived with my Mother and Grandmother on the second floor and envied Nettie.

Aunt Flora took us under her wing. We were enrolled in school, joined the Girl Scouts and were introduced to the Methodist Church in Washington Square.

Aunt Flora was a great shopper and after many an-exhausting day in the dazzling stores on Fifth Avenue we came home laden with pretty dresses and hats and gloves and such for church or other affairs.

We saw Rockefeller Center and Radio City, the

Bronx Zoo and Central Park. We learned to find our way about the city on the Sixth Avenue elevated train and the subways. We could see the Empire State Building from our rooftop rising tallest among the tall buildings of the city. We climbed to the crown of the Statue of Liberty on Staten Island. The stairs go up the inside of the statue— around and around a central pillar. The stairs up the arm had been closed for repairs. It was a tremendous view of the city from the crown. I'm not sure I would have been brave enough to have gone up the arm and viewed the city from the upraised torch in the statue's hand. We also saw the great museums. Aunt Flora saw to it that we saw many of New York City's *famous places.*

One day after school I decided to walk a block over from my usual way home. I wasn't aware that the streets fanned out and led me away from my familiar territory. So I saw *The Bowery* too—a notorious area. Ragged, decrepit, hopeless looking men slumped in entryways. I made a hasty retreat back to known streets. I longed for Orville and the Cariboo's uncluttered spaces. I suppose I poured out my unhappiness in letters to Orville. Mother added her dislike of New York and her desire to return to the Cariboo.

When my Girl Scout Leader and the Church Deaconess and a few others heard we were planning on returning to the unsettled far distant northwestern corner of Canada which most didn't even know existed—they tried to dissuade us. They sounded as if they thought the natives were still prowling about in loincloths with bows and arrows.

They reminded me of how many opportunities I was giving up. How my talents could be developed—how much more the city had to offer me.

The first 25 heifers.

Gesticulating with an arm to the great city around us they said, *"You would leave all this—for an undeveloped wilderness?"*

"Yes! Yes! I certainly would!" But I only thought it.

During our one year stay in New York Orville had quit his ranch job and started ranching on his own 160-acre pre-emption—with 25 heifers. His ranching was not making any money as yet. He also cut ties for the railway.

One 500-tie contract was all one person would be granted but you could sometimes buy a contract from someone else.

Orville did two contracts that winter—camping out in a tent where the ties were cut. Often it was -30 to -40 Degrees Fahrenheit.

A broad axe was used to hack the ties flat on two sides. They were then cut to the required length, hauled to the railway siding and stacked there.

More money was made from fur trapping. Even so—Orville left for New York in his old Chev Coupe with only $300.00 in his pocket—and without a spare tire! He had never seen a traffic light.

Ten days later, on the third of July, he arrived at the Holland Tunnel, an entrance into Manhattan.

Traffic was pouring out of the tunnel four lanes wide—bumper to bumper. New York City was preparing to celebrate the Fourth of July—Independence Day. Orville thought, *"How am I ever going to get across to the lane going into the city?"*

While he pondered, a policeman came and stopped the traffic, letting him into the lane going into the city.

Once through the tunnel he was—in Manhattan, the heart of New York City. Being somewhat overwhelmed by this time he drew into the curb and parked. A policeman, noticing the BC licence came and asked if he needed some help. Orville asked to be directed to a garage where he could store his car and take a cab to our address.

The policeman (unknowingly) directed him to the very garage where my uncle stored his *meat delivery van.* Looking at the address Orville gave him—he said it was only a few blocks from the garage and that he could walk there.

Imagine our surprise when we found Orville ringing the doorbell.

Imagine Orville's surprise when the next morning he awoke to the sound of cowbells!

Hurrying to the window, he looked down on the vegetable vendors pushing their carts along the street. It took a minute or two to notice the cowbell tied to a rope across the top of each cart.

Orville had asked the garage where he had stored his car—to check it over. They informed him he'd better trade it off for another—that it would never make it back to Canada. Orville did not have the where-with-all to do that.

A week later, Orville, Mother and I, in the same car were headed homeward—well back to the Cariboo anyway. Nettie had begged to stay with Uncle Joe and Aunt Flora.

It was a beautiful trip—the June skies smiled on us. We spent a few days in Yellowstone Park. Often we camped in the yards of country schools. They were pleasant places, uncrowded by other tourists and being summer vacation time no one seemed to care or even notice.

Mother was happy. She had escaped New York. I was ecstatically happy to be with Orville again.

In less than three weeks we were back in the Cariboo—not having had so much as a flat tire in the way of car trouble.

It was haying time. Orville and I both got a job in the hay fields. I was proud of my skill with the horse-rake.

That fall we applied for a marriage licence. We were told that for a girl under 16 to marry, consent was required from both parents—separated or not—*and a county judge*. I was 14. My father certainly wasn't going to give his consent. Mother would.

We went to see the county judge. He arranged a private hearing with my parents, Orville and I. He overruled my father's refusal and gave his consent. However he also said we must wait until I was 15—which would be in the spring of '36.

That winter Orville again cut two railway tie contracts.

The 25 heifers were being wintered in a group of wild meadows some 12 miles from where Mother and I lived—on Orville's pre-emption. The heifers would have their first calves in the spring.

Orville's tie cutting job where he camped was about 12 miles in the other direction. Orville came home on weekends and with the team and sleigh went out to the meadows and hauled a big load of hay out for the heifers. In the middle of the week I rode out and threw more hay over the stack-yard fence for them.

Orville had a muskrat trapline between the meadows the heifers were wintering in and home. He blazed a trail of marked trees—made by slashing a bit of bark off one side—to guide me into the muskrat swamps so I could check the traps on my way back from feeding heifers.

So the winter passed and the spring of 1936 came—and my fifteenth birthday. We could *now* get our licence to marry.

In the parlour of the manse the minister performed the ceremony, reminding Orville that it was customary to *pay the pastor*. We still had enough money to manage a week's honeymoon—and pay a neighbour to stay with Mother. Fortunately the old coupe was still chugging along, and gave us no extra costs or we would have had to hitchhike home.

No matter—we were together and together we could conquer the world.

Wedding—May 6th, 1936.

After our honeymoon sitting on the same
ole '28 Chevrolet Coupe that wasn't
expected to make it back to
Canada from New York.

CHAPTER II

Those Coarse Blue Overalls

I received a letter from Judge Calder, thanking me for a photograph I had sent him with his appreciation for our remembering what he had done for us. He offered this bit of advice in a postscript: *"One of the things for a woman in life is to be always tidy and dainty, so please never wear those coarse blue overalls. F.C."*

I hope he will forgive me for I spent a good part of my life in *those coarse blue overalls*—or jeans—a reasonable facsimile.

How times had changed. I asked an older ranch wife what she had worn when raking hay with a horse drawn rake.

"Long skirts," she said.

"It's a wonder you never got tangled up and killed," I remarked. Remembering the runaways I had survived—particularly the one where the rake wound up in the middle of the pond and the team in the far corner of the field. Well broke horses were scarce items for us. I could only assume they drove very dull *old* horses. It would have been hazardous to *abandon ship* in a long skirt.

CHAPTER III

Excerpts From Orville's Memoirs
(as told by Marie)

Orville woke up one morning when he was about five and was not able to find his father or little sister. He looked all about the little sod house on the vast Saskatchewan prairie. Then he saw his father walking up the path. His sister was with him.

He took them to a large orphanage. There were many children. They slept in a large room full of cots. They all ate at one large table.

Orville and his sister clung to each other for comfort in this strange place.

Then Orville became very ill and was sent to a hospital for a long time.

He learned later that he had had pleurisy pneumonia. His lung had been operated on which left a deep scar in his rib cage.

Finally he was taken back to the orphanage and reunited with his sister.

However in a short while his father returned and took Orville away with him.

Orville was terribly sad to leave his little sister behind.

Orville was left with many different families. He felt that most people didn't consider him worth feeding.

Then his father left him with an older couple

(whose 2 sons were grown up). He lived with them on a dairy farm in the Fraser River Valley of BC.

He was small and sickly so no one thought of sending him to school, but he was a handy little choreboy anxious to prove himself useful, and thus worth feeding.

Mrs. Jake was very good to him—doctoring his many and varied illnesses. Under her ministering hand and good food he became stronger, and she started him in school.

They had not heard from his father at all, and Jake and Mrs. Jake were wondering what to do with Orville because they had decided to go ranching in the Cariboo Region of BC.

By the time they were ready to leave and still had not heard from Orville's father they decided to take him with them.

He was overjoyed when he heard that he was to go with them. In a Model-T Ford they moved to the Cariboo. Orville felt he had a home at last.

There were many chores in their new location. In the evenings Orville brought the milk cow in from the unfenced rangeland and milked her then gathered wood for fires. There were endless jobs that he could help with.

He was a happy boy to be able to do these things.

This new ranch became what was termed *'Their Home Place'*, where the new log-house and barn and other buildings were. Some hay was put up for a small flock of sheep and the milk cow was now kept in a fenced pasture. Chickens and pigs were kept to supply meat and eggs. A garden supplied vegetables.

However, to be able to raise beef cattle and to build a ranch as they intended when they moved to the cariboo, they needed more hay.

There were some more hay meadows about five miles from *The Homeplace*. These could be leased, bought or pre-empted for a small fee.

So it was at seven years old Orville began the process of learning the ranching business.

CHAPTER IV

A Master's Degree
(As told in Orville's words)

Jake, my foster father was a large ruddy-cheeked formidable looking man. He had a handle bar mustache, a thick thatch of white hair and an *I conquer all* air about him. We lived on a remote ranch in the interior of British Columbia. There I had a very different education than most boys. There was no school for me to go to. But I did indeed become very well educated in matters that would become very useful to me in coping with life, as I was to find it.

In my fifteenth year, Jake built a cabin at *The Meadows*. This was where the cattle were wintered. It saved hauling hay with horses and sleigh five or six miles to *The Home Place*. For the next five years I became, during the long winter months, the lone *Keeper of the Cows*. I think back on it now and understand that I was enrolled in the initial course of Coping with Cows, leading to a *Masters Degree in Wheeling and Dealing in the Cow Business*. I was quite unaware of it then.

When I moved into the new cabin that first year, in early October, snow was already covering the ground. By the end of November the snow was so deep it required a four-horse team driven down the trail to the haystacks to break a road over which I could get a load of hay out to the 100 and some hungry cattle.

Orville, *Jake's Keeper of the Cows.*

In this bleak snow-covered world I felt like I was the only living person in the universe. The responsibility of getting the cattle fed weighed heavily on me. To make matters worse, extreme cold set in. The temperature dropped into the -40's and lower. I struggled with my job as *Keeper of the Cows*, through October—November—December—January and February. March with longer daylight hours, milder weather and summer to look forward to brought a much brighter outlook.

But busy summer days flew by and the long lonely winter rolled in again.

I became more adept, stronger and tougher, with each succeeding winter. By the time I had completed my fifth winter alone at the meadows, I believed I had passed with flying colours, the course in *Coping with Cows*. The cows had increased to two or three hundred head by then.

It was time for me to leave—as I had told Jake I would the year I was 20.

Jake discouraged my leaving, telling me I was too small, puny and uneducated to find work. Nevertheless, feeling sad and lonely, with nothing but my saddle horse and gear, I left.

In a near-by community I went to work for the *Double-Circle Ranch*. There were other young people about and I enjoyed the social life. It was during the four years I spent there that I met Marie, my wife to be. She was still a schoolgirl, but I decided I was going to wait for her to grow up.

While waiting for Marie to grow up I moved to my 160-acre pre-emption. I had bought 25 heifer calves and needed to put up hay for them. Also to obtain a Crown Grant, one was required to build a house and barn, live on the property and do certain improvements.

Orville, (second from left) with cowboys on the ranch
where he worked.

These things I set about doing.

I knew my pre-emption would never run more than
50 cattle.

"If I could find a place to run on a share basis," I
thought, *"I could increase my herd, and then, perhaps find
a ranch to buy."*

Jake heard of my plans and wanting to retire he
offered me his place to run—on a share basis—with 125
cows. I was to add my 25 cows to the herd, pay all
expenses and receive two-thirds of the combined calf crop.

He would leave me the horses and machinery
necessary for operating. At the end of five years I was to
return cattle and equipment in the condition I had received
them.

"Perhaps," he said tantalisingly, *"I vill sell it to you."*

Marie and I were married by then and we talked it over, and decided to accept the offer. It seemed like just what we were looking for. I knew it was possible to increase the herd. Jake had nearly 300 when I left in 1930. Having accepted the offer; we asked for a contract.

"Vell, vright now ve are busy mit movink," Jake said, *"unt you should get moved hin unt look hafter dese cows."*

It was the middle of the calving season so we moved in knowing—the cattle did need watching.

However I was uneasy about it. I had seen Jake deal before, and should have known better. He reassured me, in his usual convincing manner, that as soon as we were moved in he would write up the contract and sign it. One urgent matter followed another. The contract remained unwritten.

To raise money for the first years operating costs I had sold my pre-emption. However our operating costs were minimal. Marie worked long hours with me—haying and various other jobs. We didn't need to hire any help. Machinery costs were next to nothing. I had been operating and repairing this sort of equipment for years.

That fall we had surplus hay to sell as well so we didn't need to sell any calves for income. The herd was growing.

That fall Jake had 80 head of dry cows (cows that hadn't produced a calf) and a few two year old steers to sell above the 125 cows he had left with me. I had rounded them up off the range and offered to help him take them to market. While inspecting Jake's cattle, the buyer—Mr. Harvey—saw my calves already weaned, and on feed. He wanted to buy them too.

I told Mr. Harvey, *"Those are my calves, and not for sale."*

Jake replied, *"Mr. Harvey von't buy dese big cattle onless he gets dose calf's too."*

"They're not yours to sell," I repeated. *"I'll go talk to Mr. Harvey. He probably thinks they're your calves."*

Jake had indeed indicated that the calves were his.

I became convinced that Jake had no intention of drawing up that promised contract.

I was to drive the cattle Jake had for sale to the stockyards with the help of another rider. We had made arrangements to feed and water and overnight them at the Indian Reserve about 15 miles away. The next morning we were to drive them on to the stockyards—another five miles.

It was a cold November morning when we drove the herd out the gate the next day, and there wasn't much daylight left when we corralled them at the reserve.

Jake had the cattle fed a load of hay. I pulled the saddles off the horses, fed them, and I was just going to find myself a meal when along comes Mr. Harvey.

"Saddle up," says he, *"We've made a new deal. We're moving the cattle to the stock yards—tonight."*

"But, they've not had a chance to eat or drink all day! It will be dark before we even get started." With that I stomped off to speak to Jake and try to talk him out of this stupid idea.

"Mr. Harvey has offered to veigh dese cattle at 8:00 in de morning," Jake explained. *"He'll pay the tree unt half cents like ve agreed and not take tree per cent off for shrinkage. It hiss a better deal."*

The deal between Jake and Mr. Harvey was… Mr.
Harvey would pay Jake three and a half cents per pound of
his cattle's weight upon arrival at the stockyards.
Usually three percent of the cattle's weight is deducted
because they are usually full of water and feed. Mr.
Harvey was agreeing not to deduct the usual three-percent.

*"That's because he knows they'll be shrunk a lot
more than three per cent by the time we get them there,"* I
scornfully predicted.

But Jake's mind was made up. We found another
rider to help, and started out.

The cattle were going down the road surprisingly
well until Mr. Harvey, with Jake beside him, drove up
behind the herd. The car lights blinded the cattle and they
began to mill about. We were having a very difficult time
keeping them together.

It was then that I realised that Mr. Harvey had Jake
half drunk. He was deliberately causing all the trouble he
could in order to cause the cattle to lose even more weight.

It was close to midnight before we finally got the
cattle into the stockyards.

"Well they'll be veighed at eight in de mornink,"
thought Jake. *"A few hours restink von't make dat much
difference."*

However, Mr. Harvey had a few more tricks up his
sleeve. He didn't get to the stockyards until 10:00 AM.
He took one look at the cattle and exploded, "These aren't
the cattle I saw at the ranch!" And said to his son, "Pete,
cut out the good ones." This means he only intends to buy
the best ones or to cut the price on some.

*"Dere iss no cut, Mr. Harvey. Remember, tree unt
haf cents straight across mit no shrink."*

"Yes, but these aren't the cattle I saw. You wouldn't

expect me to pay three and a half cents for these! Would you?"

"Mr. Harvey, ven you vern't so olt unt crippled up I vood mop up de corral mit you. Dere vill be no cuts or I vill sue you!"

"I don't want your cattle at all," retorted Mr. Harvey. *"Come on Pete, let's go."*

Jake tried a new approach, *"I ben tinken, hit's voolish for us old buggers to be vighten. Vy don't ve veigh dese cattle? Dey lost a lot uf veight gettin here, so you know tree unt haf cent iss goot buy."*

"Don't want your cattle," snapped Mr. Harvey. *"But..."* he considers, *"I'll give you two and a half cents."*

Jake accepted. There didn't seem to be any alternative.

As I listened to these wiley old-timers trying to out-swindle each other, I knew I had made a mistake in getting involved with Jake again.

Now it was my turn to wheel and deal with Jake. I knew he was not going to willingly give me that promised contract.

Before my share of the first years calf crop could go out on the range, in the spring, they would have to be branded. I couldn't put my brand on them with nothing to show ownership. When spring came, I notified Jake that I was branding them and needed the contract signed. He ignored me. I branded the calves with his brand. Upon hearing that he came to see me.

"You should not haf done dat," he complained, *"I don't vant my brand ont your cattle. Now I vill haf to pay you for putting up da hay. I vus yust too busy to get dat contract drawn up,"* he finished.

I knew things were going just the way he wanted.

I expected he would claim the calves, offer me a pittance for wages, and try to squirm out of that.

But I didn't think his position was as good as he thought. I had paid all operating costs, and wage earners don't do that.

Meanwhile, I had heard that Jake's son, Bill, wanted to take on the ranch.

I was surprised, but I knew that at a time that seemed opportune to him, I would hear about it.

My informant told me, *"They're going to let you put up the hay and then take the ranch back. I know you think you've got a five year deal, so I thought you should know."*

That summer I put up just enough hay to see Jake's cattle, and mine, through the winter and used the other meadows for pasture.

This news reached Jake. *"I hear you haf vinished hayink,"* he commented.

"Yes," I replied, *"I've enough to winter on. I can save the cost of putting up more."* Adding, *"The other meadows will make good fall pasture."*

"I tink you petter put it up," Jake advised, *"You nefer know vut kind uff vinter comes."*

"I've enough," I repeated. *"If I need more I'll buy some. It's my problem."*

When he heard I had turned the horses out and put the haying equipment away he knew I wasn't going to put up anymore hay.

A week later he came back. *"I don't know vut to do about dis deal mit you,"* he said. *"Bill vants to haf dis place. I don't know vut to do mit you."*

"That's no problem," I assured him, *"If Bill wants the place, let him have it. All I want is the calves, as*

promised, and enough hay to winter my cattle. As soon as you draw up that promised contract I'll move, but I think the sensible thing to do would be to let me feed your cattle and mine 'til spring. We'd have completed two years according to our deal, and I'd have the summer to look for a place for my cattle."

Jake said he'd go talk to Bill about it. Next day a letter informed me that Bill wanted to take over right away, and would be moving in in six days. Would I move out so he could have the house? Then he'd come settle with me for taking care of the cattle and the place. Six days later two trucks loaded with furniture were in the yard. Bill was asking, *"Didn't you get Dad's letter?"*

"Yep, I got it," I replied.

"Well how come you haven't moved?" Bill wanted to know.

"I'll move when Jake signs the contract I was supposed to get two years ago, when I moved in. Go tell him I'm not moving until I have that contract, signed, as promised."

"What am I going to do with my furniture, it might rain?" Bill wailed.

"That's your problem," I commented.

"Is Dad's word no good?" asked Bill indignantly. *"He said he'd settle with you as soon as I get moved in. We're too busy now. Winter's close you know."*

"If Jake's word was any good I'd have had that contract signed two years ago."

Angrily, Bill piled his furniture outside and left.

Jake was there early the next morning. *"Didn't you get my letter?"* he asked.

"Yes, I did." I replied, *"I'll move when you sign our agreement."*

"It's my house," Jake roared, *"I vill trow you out."*

"I'll move as soon as you draw up and sign our agreement," I repeated. *"I've found a vacant place just four miles away where I can winter."*

"Bill, draw up dat contract." Snapped Jake.

After some arguments over the wording of the contract—we both signed it.

I took my cattle and household goods and moved. By then it was getting too cold to brand my share of the second years calf crop.

When spring came Jake informed me that I had better not brand those calves until I had a bill of sale for them. He didn't think the contract he had signed was valid.

I branded the calves with my iron—confident that the contract was valid.

Jake told his lawyer that I had branded some of his calves.

I explained to the lawyer that I had a contract giving me ownership of the calves I had branded.

He said, *"Jake never told me. I'll see him about it."*

Next, I heard from the brand inspector. *"Jake tells me you have a bunch of his calves you claim, but don't own, and not to clear them until you show a bill of sale. I thought I'd tell you now so you can get one. I can't pass them if you can't show ownership."*

I showed him my signed agreement.

"That's all you need," he smiled, *"Bring 'em all in."*

I figured I had just received my Masters Degree in Wheeling and Dealing in the Cow Business.

CHAPTER V

Outgrowing Our First Ranch

When the lease with Jake was terminated, due to his son Bill taking Jake's ranch over, we had no place to go. It was fall. Bill wanted the ranch immediately. We had to find a place where the cattle could be wintered.

If we were to use our share of the hay that we had put up that summer, we would need a place to winter within a reasonable distance to the hay.

Jake had sold his *old home place* to a man who couldn't meet his payments. This was the place where Orville had grown up. It was only four miles from the meadows that we had been leasing.

Orville went to see this man and found he needed 100 dollars to meet his due payment and that Jake was threatening forclosure.

We bought the place for 600 dollars—100 and a horse for the down payment—and no interest on the balance. *"It's my money,"* Orville argued, *"so why should I pay interest on it."* The sellar seemed unable to refute this logic.

Jake was pretty upset when he found Orville had short-circuited his expectations of getting his original home ranch back.

Now we had a ranch plus 25 cows, 100 calves, about 100 yearlings, and a beautiful baby girl—Iris.

Glad as we were to get the place, it represented

another challenge. The ranch had not been lived on for several years and resembled a disaster area.

The house was made of logs mudded over inside with a willow lathe arrangement to hold the mud-and-hog-bristle-plaster. It had two rooms downstairs and three attic rooms reached by ladder-like stairs. Floors were rough boards. Pack rats had been living there for some time and had big smelly lodges made of twigs and trash constructed in the corners. Rats are more odorous than skunks in as much as they never *turn it off*. A skunk only smells when alarmed.

Needless to say, this place took a bit of cleaning up—hastened by the fact that winter was close. The rat smell faded gradually but we couldn't get it completely out of the mud-plaster.

Our new home place didn't have enough hay for the cattle. Orville found a group of meadows eight miles away. For these he paid 350 dollars—and a bull. In October of '38 we put up a cabin there in 10 days.

It was lovely that first winter in our new cabin with its unpeeled logs—cracks chinked with fresh moss and warmed with a wood stove—and love.

Succeeding years were another story. When the bark on the logs dried, bugs moved in burrowing their little trails through the wood. The moss dried every year and needed to be redone—*if* we moved in before winter to do it. We usually didn't. Fresh cow manure slapped on the outside had to do. It really wasn't *that* bad. It made a tight seal and when frozen left no noticeable smell.

The years flew by. In the spring of '39 our second daughter *Janet* was born and in the fall of '40 another girl—*Gail*. My mother was still with us so when the chores and feeding were done Orville and I often went squirrel hunting. The fur was worth as much as one dollar a pelt and we would get 10 to 20 dollars or even 30 dollars on some days—big money in the '30's. With this extra money I bought a big square of linoleum, curtain material and heavy building-paper and paint for the home place. I managed to make the building paper stick to the horrible mud walls with a boiled flour paste with some flakes of glue melted in it and *inspiration indeed*—some cinnamon, which helped with the smell. No woman could have been more pleased with the results.

In 1943, Iris, our first born was six years old. The nearest school was seven miles away. Too far for her to ride a horse. Besides, in winter, we were at the meadow cabin, a good twelve miles from 150 Mile House—and usually snowed in. I enrolled Iris in the Government Correspondence School.

In 1945 Janet and Gail joined our homeschool class. Although Gail was only five, I thought it would be easier if she started also rather than me trying to cope with three grades. Unsure of myself, and anxious for my girls to do well, I laid down a strict schedule, but we had fun too. They were good students. From November to April I rode horseback to 150 Mile House almost every week to mail and receive lessons. I can still see the welcoming lights of the coal oil lamps through the trees as I rode home in the dark.

The welcoming light shone from this window of the cabin.

Orville—*working the fields.*

Marie and Raymond.

Orville and Raymond.

Grandma Case, Orville, Baby Raymond and
girls at a summer picnic.

Grandma Case, Raymond, Iris and Gail playing in Valley Creek at *The Old Place.*

The Old Place—where Orville grew up and we eventually bought.

View from *The Old Place.*

Betty fishing in Valley Creek at *The Old Place (about 1948).*

Orville and Raymond driving haying slip. *"Startin' 'em young."*

Raymond at the *winter feeding camp.*

During these years we added a neighboring 160-acres to *Our Home Place*, cleared some land, and put it under irrigation. We also bought the hay on another place where we spent one winter.

At Christmas the girls had a ringside seat, peaking through knotholes in the upstairs floor, to watch Santa fill up their stockings. We even had a Christmas program with three performers and three spectators—Orville, Gramma Case and me.

And then there was a boy (Raymond) and some fifteen months later another girl (Betty). We were certainly ourgrowing our beginnings. We had two more children approaching school age and a cowherd outgrowing our land base. It was time to look around for another place.

CHAPTER VI

144 Mile Ranch

The 144 Mile Ranch went up for sale in the late '40's. It was dry—rocky hillsides.

"Why would you buy that pile of rocks?" was the general comment when we did just that.

We had spent the first 14 years of our marriage ranching in the *higher altitudes* of the Cariboo Country of British Columbia.

Orville had spent most of his life battling the hardships of ranching in one of the most difficult parts of the country.

This high country produced poor swamp hay— spring came late—and a short summer was followed by a long cold winter. Rangeland consisted of endless acres of jack pine forests with an occasional little swampy meadow.

If managed carefully one *could* raise cattle there, but Orville's keen blue eyes observed the difference in the livestock in the main river valleys and decided—that was the place to ranch.

When the 144 Mile Ranch in the San Jose River Valley went up for sale, he saw it as an opportunity to get out of the high country, and build a ranch in the valley— never mind if it was a pile of rocks. There were sunny dry bunch grass hillsides, a boon to calving cows, when in the higher country—mud, slush, and snow still prevailed.

There the first green grass sprouted and the deer gathered
for the early spring feast. There, the cows fed on the
sparse but nutritious bunch grass later into the winter than
they did anywhere else. There was a place to view the
valley spread out below you—to watch the glorious
sunsets fade and the sunrise touch the tree tops with gold.
These low-lying hills were called the *Spring Fields*.

The 144 Mile Ranch Headquarters were only 15
miles from town and cattle markets. A school was only
five miles away and served by a bus.

With three children enrolled in a correspondence
school, and two more children approaching school age, a
school seemed mandatory.

The problem was with the price being three times
the value of our ranch. How could we afford it? Perhaps
if we had enough time—like twenty years or so...

Orville considered the possibilities. We didn't
have *enough cattle* to make the payments. We didn't have
enough money to buy *enough cattle* to make the payments.
The ranch wasn't producing *enough hay* to feed *enough
cattle* to make the payments. But Orville looked at the
ranch's 4000 acres and envisioned water from the higher
country dramatically increasing their productivity to make
the *not enough—enough!*

He remembered the small flock of sheep he had
tended as a boy. In his *minds eye* he saw one mother ewe
with two lambs being marketed for twice her value.

We sold our first ranch and most of the cattle and
bought 700 ewes—made a very small down payment on
the 144 Mile Ranch which was priced at 30,000 dollars.
To us, in 1949, the price was a staggering amount.

144 Mile Roadhouse and barn that acccomodated gold seekers
heading for Barkerville. (the 1860's gold rush town).

Highway '97 looking North from *144 Mile Ranch House*
when it was still a winding gravel and dirt road.

The Big Meadow Cabin at the far end of the *144 Mile Ranch* as we wind up the haying season. Our oldest daughter Iris and the two younger ones sitting on *Blacky*.

CHAPTER VII

From Roadhouse to Ranch Home

With the ranch came the roadhouse that had served in the 1860's as a stopping place for the miners and adventurers who were flocking to the booming gold rush town of Barkerville.

A road had been built from the Port City of Vancouver, BC where the Fraser River meets the Pacific Ocean. Up the awesome Fraser River canyon, the road hung on trestles from the rock walls and twisted up side canyons and bridged tumultuous mountain streams. Up this road adventurers and dreamers came from everywhere—headed for the fabulously rich gold fields of Barkerville.

At Lillooet, where the Fraser meets the North Thompson, the Cariboo Trail begins—winding through the dry hills and gulches of the interior and pushing northward through bogs and thick spruce forests—on to Barkerville.

To supply food and lodging to travelers, roadhouses sprang up along the trail. They were named according to the miles from Lillooet—thus 144 Mile Roadhouse.

In 1949 the character and faded glory of this old roadhouse still lingered. But as a ranch house and family home it left much to be desired.

The upstairs bedrooms still had the numbers on the doors—*one to six*.

144 Mile Roadhouse.

They were small rooms each with one deep dormer window.

They were hot in summer and cold in winter. The gable end, finished with rough boards and no insulation was *especially* cold in winter.

It wasn't long before I was knocking out those walls of one layer of boards, running up and down and covered with aged cracked wall paper, to make one large semi-divided airier room for our three oldest girls. A few sheets of plywood to build stow-a-way spots—desks and closets under the eaves that were rough, but adequate from my point of view—then some paper and paint and the stuffy little rooms became a comparatively pleasant larger room.

Some heavy felt paper to cover the rough boards on the gable-end gave a bit of insulation. But if it hadn't been for the barrel heater in the lobby below and the *klondike chimney* running through the bedroom above, the occupants would have found those minus forty degree or lower winter nights even harder to endure.

Downstairs, to the right of the lobby was a small bedroom that became our nursery. Behind it was a room that had been the family parlor. This became our bedroom.

Behind the lobby was the kitchen—by-passed by a short hall to the guests' long dining room.

The kitchen was large enough to hold a table and benches to seat at least ten people. A big wood-range and the wood-box stood beside the entry door. Beside it was a stand for the washbasin and water-bucket and—the bane of my life—a slop pail for the wastewater. That kitchen was a thorn in my flesh. A door in the middle of every wall made it impossible to arrange any work area.

"Look Honey," I coaxed Orville for the umpteenth time. *"If we moved that partition back three or four feet I could have a work centre that would hold everything I need in one place. The sink could go there."*

"What sink?" Orville moved indifferently out the door. Ranchers are not usually concerned with household matters.

A stove, a table, benches, a few shelves—a stand for the water bucket and basin and underneath our disposal system—*the obnoxious slop pail*. This was a completely furnished kitchen. A wife who thought it was not adequate soon discovered there were *more important things* to deal with.

One morning *the boss* rode off to attend to some of *those more important things* at the far meadow—and didn't plan on returning for two or three days.

He hadn't got out of sight before I had hammer and wrecking bar out and was *attacking* that wall.

It was only a single layer of upright boards nailed to a board along the floor and another along the ceiling. It wasn't long before I had the whole thing down.

Then I started to put those boards upright a few feet farther over, and they were too long. The old ceiling had sunk several inches where it earlier had been held up by the partition. I was contemplating how I will deal with this problem when in the kitchen door walks *the boss.*

I can't remember all that he said. I guess that one's memory is sometimes mercifully blank. However the remarks ended with *"Wel-l-l—where do you want it?"*

I gratefully said, *"About here,"* and held boards in place while he measured, sawed—and grumbled.

Next day he was again off to attend those things having asked as he gave me a good-bye hug, *"Would you change the turn-outs on the irrigation in the Spring Field?"*

Having attended to that chore I proceeded to build counters and shelving. I was quite pleased with my arrangement even if it didn't have doors or arborite top. After a good paint job, it looked all right to me.

Later we found a dandy old cast-iron enameled sink. It even had double-drain boards. True it didn't yet have taps or drains. But the horrid old slop pail had a hiding place even if it did sometimes get forgotten—and overflowed.

In due time the water did come from taps and ran out drains.

The little path to the four-seater outhouse—the relic of the gold rush days—grew dim. The long dining room became a bedroom, a bathroom, and next to the kitchen a laundry room which replaced a laundry shed that froze up every winter.

The Old Roadhouse that had served the travelers in the gold rush days of the 1860's had taken on a new character in the 1950's.

CHAPTER VIII

The Sheep and Why

We had one employee, Joe—a small willing man who had helped us during the haying season for some years. He knew very little about livestock but always had our best interests at heart. We left the sheep in Joe's care and went on a two-day trip to buy rams for the flock. Fortunately the ram purchases went smoothly. We were back early the second day.

Joe was desperate. *"Somting's madder widda sheep,"* he reported, *"Whole bunch can't get up."*

"Did you put them in the alfalfa?" Orville questioned.

"Ya," said Joe, *"No feed on dose hills."*

Joe had noticed how poor the feed on the hillsides looked as compared to the harvested alfalfa fields. He opened the gate and let the sheep in.

Sheep, accustomed to hard grass, will gorge themselves on such lush pasture and bloat and die.

"They've bloated on that alfalfa," Orville informed Joe, *"Take the dogs and get them moving—as many as you can."*

Then Orville began to tie sticks across the tongues of the ones unable to get up. This caused them to belch up gas, enabling them—with some heavy-handed urging—to struggle to their feet and join the moving flock.

It was a close call. All our resources were tied up

in those sheep and many were in danger of dying.

Joe had one phrase when things went wrong.

"Damn tings," he fumed, *"Damn tings."*

But he stayed on, faithfully helping—*and advising.*

That winter required a careful marshalling of funds. Our resources were almost non-existent, but we were used to making do. The cellar was stocked with vegetables from our garden. The woods supplied deer and moose meat. Then a cheque for wool at shearing time recharged our bank account.

Orville was concerned about the condition of the ewes. They had come off a poor range the summer before. Also they were getting past their prime and they had gone into winter far too thin.

How good a lamb crop would we get?

Six weeks before the lambs were due the ewes began delivering pre-maturely. The vet recommended cod liver oil mixed with bran to restore their vitamin D deficiency, which was causing the pre-mature deliveries. It cured the problem. We shipped a 110% lamb crop that fall.

Although the lamb crop could have been better, we had cleared 7000 dollars more the first year than we had paid for the ewes and rams.

That fall, a wool company offered one dollar a pound for the spring-shearing backed up by a contract with a down payment.

This was an unprecedented rise in wool prices. The agriculturist advised us against the contract.

"The company knows the price will be higher by shearing time. Hang in there. You'll get more," he confidently predicted.

Orville replied, *"I never thought I'd see wool at a*

dollar a pound. That's good enough for me."

By shearing time the price had dropped.

Our second lambing season started in late March and continued through April. A night watchman penned ewe and lambs as they arrived—saw that the lambs nursed and made the rounds again, usually bringing in another set or two.

This lambing season the ewes were in good condition and a bumper crop of lambs was arriving. This presented problems. Quite a number of older ewes didn't have enough milk for twins.

Every morning and evening I checked the new arrivals. Then I turned them into their respective areas. Ewes with twins that had enough milk and ewes with singles went into the main feeding area.

Ewes that seemed unlikely to raise twins were marked so I knew which ones belonged to which mother. If one began to fail I put it in my bummer-pen and turned the ewe with one lamb into the main feeding area. A bummer is a lamb or calf whose mother doesn't supply enough milk. They will try to get milk from other mothers.

My bummer-pen grew unmanageable. There wasn't enough time. We were all too busy.

Soon I was advertising, *"New Born Lambs to Give Away."*

I poured out my woes to unheeding ears.

The men knew there was only one answer. They would knock the extra one on the head. Since I hadn't listened to them it was my problem.

I already had over a dozen lambs in my bummer pen and some of them weren't doing very well. I had to do *something.*

I couldn't take care of them all and no one wanted anymore lambs.

However, being a hopeful sort, I kept hoping that the odd ewes that sometimes lost their lambs would be glad to adopt one. But lambing was almost over and there were no spare mothers.

Well...I found a stout club and sorted out the scrubbier ones and did what the men recommended.

I kept six. With the children's help—I could manage. The others I knocked on the head.

Then I went to prepare the bottles for the six that were left.

When I returned they were *all* on their feet bleating for their bottles. I returned to the house and got the .22 rifle and finished the job and cried as I continued my chores.

Betty, Ladybug and Raymond.

Iris, Janet and Gail with their pet lambs.

Iris feeding *Ladybug*. Ladybug never knew she was a sheep and
remained a member of the family for years.

The family (1950) at *144 Mile Ranch*.
(Gail, Iris, Marie, Betty, Raymond, Orville and Janet).

The lambs I spared became the children's pets.
Among them was one special very tiny one. They called
her *Ladybug*. She had a woolly brown face and brown
legs. She looked like a toy, especially when shampooed
and beribboned. She followed them everywhere—into the
kitchen for raisins and rolled oats snacks and down to the
river for swimming. She wasn't very good at that; her
wool got water logged and she'd have to be pulled out.

To watch the flock, a few weeks after lambing, was
a delightful sight. One lamb would jump up on a high
spot, give a wiggly little leap, jump off, and run. All eight
or nine hundred would follow each doing the same thing,

playing follow the leader—it seemed.

When they all got racing round and round, the whole hillside seemed to be moving.

Into these pleasant scenes came another aspect—*predator kills*. Sheep are vulnerable to coyotes, cougars, bears and wolves. The presence of a large flock of sheep drew them in. There were some losses.

Coyotes were the most numerous. Orville reduced their numbers by 70 in two years. Five *sheep-eating cougars* and *eight bears* also fell to his hunting skills. At that time a bounty was paid for these predators, who were considered too numerous.

Camping with the sheep near
the Cougar's Domain—*The Spruce Swamp*

Sheep-eating Cougar.

The haystooks.

Marie, on the slip.

Building *the haystack.*

During haying we camped in the Jones Creek
Valley where there was a cabin where we ate and the
children slept. This was where the ranch's main
hay-meadows were.

In order to keep a night watch Orville and I had a
camp on an old truck that we moved to wherever the
sheep were bedding down. If anything disturbed the
sheep—we would know.

One night Orville went away and I was night
watchman.

I looked out on a peaceful scene. The sheep were
bedded down on the crest of a hill. Moonlight highlighted
their soft wooly backs. Cloud shadows drifted over them.
Below lay a spruce swamp. All was peaceful and
beautiful in the moonlight.

I snuggled down in bed but just as I was dozing off

a chorus of yapping and howling brought me wide awake.

The flock bleated here and there—uneasily. I decided I would take a stroll through that swamp and scare those coyotes away. Taking the .22 rifle from the wall, but not bothering to dress, I headed out.

As I approached the swamp the howling ceased. I walked farther in—fired my gun a couple of times—listened—heard nothing, and decided to go back to bed. *"I'll have scared them off for now,"* I reasoned.

Then across a patch of moonlight I glimpsed a shadowy form slinking away.

The next day I reported to Orville, "The coyotes were sure noisy last night, and I think there might be something dead in the swamp."

Orville went to investigate.

"But it's not a coyote-kill," he said, *"It's cougar."*

"Oh Yi, Yi!" I exclaimed, *"I was walking in that swamp in my nightshirt, in the middle of the night . . . with cougars!"*

Orville laughed.

CHAPTER IX

The Options

That fall, when our second crop of lambs was ready for sale, Orville considered the options.

The price of sheep had gone up. The ewes were past their peak production years. The sale of the entire flock would bring us enough to pay off the ranch mortgage and possibly a start at restocking the place with *cattle*.

"A bird in hand..." mused Orville and decided to sell the entire flock.

Ladybug mysteriously dissapeared and reappeared later. Of course Ladybug was not part of the flock.

The sheep were to be delivered to Ashcroft. The closest Railway Terminal going east to Alberta.

The old P.G.E. Railway, locally known as the *Please Go Easy* would take the sheep to Clinton. From there a trail drive of about three days would take them to Ashcroft.

They were to arrive in Clinton very early in the morning. We would meet them with the ranch truck loaded with a camp outfit, and a saddle horse. Our two oldest girls came along to help with the drive.

We arrived immediately after the train-crew had shunted the cars full of sheep onto a siding. They had banged the cars together in the process hard enough to break down a top deck.

Sheep at the 144—1949-51.

The sheep on the bottom were smothering. Had we been a few minutes later many would have been dead.

The side door was quickly forced open, and the sheep tumbled out, stunned but ready to go. The rest were unloaded, and soon the flock of over *fifteen hundred sheep* was moving down Highway 97—toward Ashcroft.

Orville rode up and down through the flock helping motorists through. One motorist busy taking pictures didn't understand. He was quite perturbed when he asked how long we would be on the road, and was told about three days.

"But we have a baby in the car. We can't be that long on the road!" he protested.

"The rider will be back shortly and help you through," we reassured him.

Ashcroft lay in a canyon along the North Thompson River. The road branched above Ashcroft. One road took a longer, gentler route down to the village.

The other wound down steep canyon walls. There wasn't room enough for cars to go through without danger of crowding the sheep off the road.

If cars would just take the longer route we could be in Ashcroft before nightfall and save another day on the trail.

The police said if we could put a man to direct traffic at the top fork, they would put one at the Ashcroft end.

A friend, Marvin, who lived in the area, agreed to direct traffic at the top. Sheep were not popular in this area. Marvin hated sheep. But some friends are always friends.

We started the flock down the steep-canyon-road. There was nowhere for sheep or cars to travel but on the narrow two-lane road.

I was following the flock in the truck. Orville, on horseback, was patrolling the outer edge. All seemed under control. Then a carload full of young men pulled up behind me. I continued down the middle of the road preventing them from passing me.

"Those sheep have no right to be blocking the road," they said, *"and we're going through."*

Our traffic director, Marvin, showed up about then, squeezed recklessly by them, and drew up beside me. I had been going very slowly—pausing often to let the sheep keep ahead.

"They won't listen to me," Marvin complained, *"I left a sign directing traffic the other way. If we drive side by side, they'll just have to stay behind."*

The car full of young men turned around and left.

We were continuing slowly onward when a little old rattletrap truck came roaring up through the sheep.

Marvin, a hot headed fellow, jumped out and stalked over to the little truck, threatening to pull the man out and knock his teeth down his throat. The man got out of his truck, pulled his teeth out and laid them on the seat.

Fortunately, Orville, having followed the truck through the sheep arrived on the scene.

"Oh, let him go Marvin. He's through now. Just move your truck and let him get out of here," he advised.

Marvin went to move his truck. He told the old fellow to get the hell out of there before he filled his teeth with sheep manure and stuffed them down his throat.

We heard later that the fellow was *down on sheep* because a large flock went by his little farm every spring and fall on their way to and from their mountain range and ate up his pasture.

We arrived in Ashcroft, a small railway town and farm supply centre, early enough to pen and feed the sheep and indulge in the luxury of a bath and dinner at the hotel.

The next day the sheep were loaded onto boxcars and headed for Alberta.

Sheep at the *144 Mile Ranch*—1949-51

Family Picnic—1953. From left: Janet, Iris, Gail, Betty in front,
Raymond, Orville (holding Karen) and Grandma Case.

CHAPTER X

Irrigation Projects

Through 1952, '53 and '54 we started restocking the ranch with cattle and rebuilding an *abandoned* irrigation system on Felker Creek which had once watered the west side of the valley.

The irrigation of the *Spring Fields* and lower land along the east side of the San Jose River was still perking in Orville's mind.

He knew water could be brought to those dry hills. He proposed to dam Squawks Lake and apply for flood rights on the stored water. He would then release the stored water into Knife Creek which flowed out of Squawks Lake, and turn it into a ditch that would run five miles across country and water the Spring Fields of the 144 Mile Ranch.

He approached the water department for the regulations for applying for water rights and building dams and ditches.

He found that an engineer would be required to draw up specifications for a dam. Right-of-way for ditching over crown land would have to be approved. Down-stream water-users would have to be consulted and their consent granted for any changes that might occur in their irrigation systems.

About five miles below Squawks Lake and some twenty miles up Knife Creek was the Grey Place. The owners had water rights on Knife Creek. They also had some small meadows leased around Squawks Lake that would be flooded if the lake was dammed.

Mr. Grey was willing, when presented with the idea, to release his leases by the lake in exchange for irrigation rights for land on his homeplace.

The next property down stream was the Chisholm Place. Since the 1800's it had held water rights on Knife Creek.

Out of Knife Creek, in the center of the Chisholm Place, the ditch to the 144 Mile Ranch would have to begin. We eventually purchased the Chisholm Place.

Four or five miles farther down Knife Creek lay the 141 Mile Ranch, holder of the oldest and largest water rights on Knife Creek.

They were interested in the damming of Squawks Lake, because the flow of Knife Creek often dropped too low to irrigate in late summer or fall.

An agreement to help with the dam building in exchange for some rights to the stored water ensued.

Orville found a used TD-9 crawler tractor for sale—just what he needed for dam building and ditching.

The pipe needed for the dam became available due to the oil pipeline recently built across BC. The reject pipe was sold for a very reasonable price. It was 30 inches across and very heavy—just what was needed for the dam.

In 1956 the ditch out of Knife Creek at Chisholm was tackled. The only feasible spot out of the creek-bed was through a spring-fed spruce-swamp along a bank that kept slipping away. After pulling bogged-down machinery out of the mud numerous times, and lining the bank side of the ditch with dolomite, a compound to help seal it, they found they could get the Knife Creek water headed across country to the 144 Mile Ranch.

In '57 the remainder of the ditch was surveyed to the 144 Mile's Spring Fields, and some ditching completed.

The work on Squawk's Lake Dam began in the fall of 1958.

Due to an exeptionally dry year Knife Creek was dry where it left the lake. Some beaver had moved in and built several dams, backing the water up to make some swampy little lakes at the top end of the main lake. It was a great help to have the creek bed dry.

Orville on the TD-9 began a large cut through the bank where Knife Creek left the lake. In this cut he manoeuvered the huge pipe into place—much as an ant wriggles his treasures into an anthill.

Our neighbor on the 141 Mile Ranch brought his crawler tractor pulling what he called a *Tumble-bug*. It scooped up dirt that Fred dumped into the trench which had been made for the pipe that would carry the water out of the lake. A head gate had been installed across the pipe to control the flow of water.

A sense of urgency began to pervade the job. Freeze up was not far away.

Our oldest daughter Iris had married and her husband Dave and she came to help.

They set up a camp. Iris cooked and ran errands. Dave mixed cement in a barrel mixer, wheeled it up a ramp in a wheelbarrow, and dumped it in the frame designed to hold the head gate.

Before they were fininshed it was freezing nights. Some snow began to fall. They were glad to set the irrigation project aside until spring, but the dam was in and the spring run off would be held back for the next summer's irrigation!

Water from Knife Creek poured down the ditch in the spring of '59 headed toward those dry acres!

"Let me know when you get water running uphill in that ditch," quipped a neighbor. *"I'd like to see it!"* What he did not know was that irrigation ditches can look like they're running uphill even when they're not.

The water did have to be coaxed around a few bends, but usually it flowed gently down the ditch. What a thrill it was for Orville, with a small tractor and plough, to run the feeder ditches from the main ditch and watch the water follow his ploughed furrows down the ridges and trickle away over the ground. What a transformation that water made! In just a few years water turned some 600 acres of sparsley grassed pastureland into a lush green landscape.

An antique seeder was even employed to put some grass seed into the wet land much to the disapproval of agriculturists and farmers who told Orville he couldn't do it that way, but must plow and make a proper seed bed. But grow it did—abundantly.

The rocky spots became less obvious and the rich productive little valleys and flat spots in those fields became lush green hay fields and pastures.

In the spring, the deer came out into those fields by the hundreds, enjoying the early grass. In the timber behind those open fields snow is often a foot or more deep and crusted on top—making it difficult for the deer to run and easy for the coyotes to run them down. Those *Spring Fields* are a refuge for the deer. We enjoy watching them. A little later, with the snow in the woods gone and new grass sprouting in small openings, the deer drift back into the shelter of the timber.

Spring Fields.

CHAPTER XI

The Horse That Became Friend and Family
(Beginnings and Continuings)

One of Orville's most rewarding experiences while he was growing up with Jake was the acquiring of his first saddle horse. He rescued her from a wild band in the early spring of a long and bitterly cold winter.

She was a small colt, slowly starving to death, and he was a lonely little boy.

Jake had sent him out to see if he could spot a team that had been missing since fall. Presumably, they had joined a wild band that was now driven by hunger, and coming into meadows closer to the ranch.

Orville saw the starving colt and forgot all about the team.

He hurried home, gathered a bag of the best hay he could find, and took it to her. This he continued to do everyday.

When she began to take an interest in the hay, he coaxed her *bit-by-bit* to follow him.

Eventually, much to his joy, he had her in the ranch corrals.

He named her Dolly.

Orville had no companions. He did not even go to school. So when his chores were done he spent every spare minute with Dolly.

'Pals'

Early each morning, when he brought her the best hay he could find, he would whistle for her. Before long the whistle brought an answering nicker.

Soon he was combing out her tangled black mane, and she responding by nuzzling his tousled blonde head.

By summer Dolly was enjoying being curried from head to toe. She grew slick, beautiful and playful. Together they gamboled over the hills happy in each other's company.

By summer Orville started teaching Dolly to respond to bridle and bit. He taught her to shake hands, as dogs are often taught to do, and to paw three times when asked, *"How old are you, Dolly?"*

By late fall Orville was riding Dolly everywhere.

Dolly and Orville.

Often camping overnight, when checking his traplines, he would find her a welcome companion. There was no need to tie Dolly up to keep her with him. She'd be standing over him in the morning—or nearby—and she would come at his whistle.

The money he made from his trap line supplied him with a saddle and better bridle and bit, halter and other equipment for Dolly—Jake got the rest of it.

In 1930—Orville—now a young man of 20, and Dolly a veteran cow-horse, left their remote ranch home and took a job on a large ranch in a neighbouring community.

It was there that I met them.

Orville and Dolly, on a steep hillside near my parent's home were practising for *The Mountain Race*—a famous event at the yearly rodeo.

I was entranced by the obvious bond between this handsome young man and his horse.

When he swung down off her back and rubbed her neck, I'm sure she knew he was telling her what a great horse she was.

When the mountain race was run that year—I was there.

From the grandstand I could see the little group of horses, far up the mountainside, diminished in size by the distance—lining up for the start. A hogback, an open strip that dropped away on both sides into timber, ran down the steep face of the mountain. Down this narrow passageway the horses, vying with each other for space, would almost seem—*to fly.*

There was a well-known horse—Grey Eagle, several others—and Dolly. Grey Eagle, aptly named, had consistently won this race for many years.

Except for Grey Eagle who stood out because of his colour, I couldn't tell one horse from another at that distance.

They would be visible coming down the hogback, disappear into the trees some two-thirds of the way down, break out onto an open hillside, and sweep onto the racetrack.

I held my breath as the group sprang into action. Grey Eagle was leading.

The rest were grouped too close to see who was next. Then they spread out but again, being too far away to tell one bay horse from another, I couldn't tell who was closest to Grey Eagle.

I noticed that half way down the hogback there were fewer horses than had started the race. The few remaining disappeared for a moment into the trees, then broke out onto the open hillside. Grey Eagle was still leading, but like a shadow close behind, was a bay horse—Dolly—with Orville bent low over her neck!

The crowd rose as one—*cheering!* Was it for Grey Eagle or was it for Dolly? Both perhaps, but the cheers from me were for *'Dolly'!*

ISBN 141200926-X